St. Sophia
The Chora Church

REHBER
BASIM YAYIN DAĞITIM
REKLAMCILIK VE TİCARET A.Ş.

REVAK

ST. SOPHIA
THE CHORA CHURCH

CONTENTS

Published and distributed by:

REHBER Basım Yayın Dağıtım
Reklamcılık ve Tic. A.Ş.
Dolapdere Cad. No.106 Dolapdere-Şişli-İSTANBUL/TURKEY
Tel.: 90.212 240 58 05 • 240 72 82   Fax: 90.212 231 33 50
http:www.revak.com.tr

Photographs :
Erdal Yazıcı, Güngör Özsoy,
Dönence Diabank

Typesetting :
AS & 64 Ltd. Şti

Colour separation and Printed in Turkey by
Asır Matbaacılık A.Ş.

St. Sophia

St. Sophia, which is a museum and accessible to everyone today, is one of the most glorious monuments of the Byzantine Empire. Originally a church, St. Sophia was built in the 6th century A.D and was transformed into a mosque by the Turks after the conquest in 1453.

This building which was turned into a museum in 1935 bears both the characteristics of a church and the ones of a mosque at the same time.

It is open to visit everyday except Monday between 9.30 a.m- 4.30 p.m.

The building we have today is the third one which has been built on the area where the two former buildings also used to stand. The first church was erected by Constantine, the son of emperor Constantine; it was named the"Mega Eklesia" (the Big Church) and was inaugurated in 360 A.D. In the following years, the name of this church was turned into Hagia Sophia, that is, Holy Wisdom as it was taught

St. Sophia, a view from the Blue Mosque.

St. Sophia, aerial photograph.

by Christianity. The first building, which was a classical church with stone walls, three arch-vaults and a wooden roof, was demolished by the inhabitants' riot which burst out upon the exile of Ioannis Chrisostomos, the Patriarch of Constantinople, in 404 A.D.

The second St. Sophia was ordered to architect Ruffinos by Theodosius II. The new church had five arch-vaults and a wooden roof, and it was put to religious service in 415.

A part of the second church building which was excavated in 1935 is approximately two meters deeper than the entrance floor at the west side of the present church.

The archaeological excavations have brought various columns, Corinthian capitals and two marble friezes with lambs denoting the twelve apostles into daylight. The second church was also burned down and demolished during a public upheaval which was named the "Revolt of Nika" after the rebels shouting, "Nika!" (Victory!).

This rebellion took place in 532 under the rule of Justinianus.

It burst out during the regular horse races and had many political and religious reasons. The revolt was organized by the emperor's nephews who had planned to dethrone him. St. Sophia was one of the many buildings which were burned down during the riots which lasted six days.

After commander Belisarius had a lot of

St. Sophia, the central building and outside views from the Fosatti Collection, XIX. century.

people killed, emperor Justinianus ordered the construction of the third and final St. Sophia.

The architects of the final church were Antemios of Tralles and Isidorus of Miletos. Construction began on 23 February 532 and ended on 27 December 537, that is, it took only five years, ten months and four days to complete it.

Hundred masters and tens of thousands of workers worked at the construction of the church. Because Justinianus had wanted the most glorious of all churches, precious materials were brought to the city from many different areas of the empire.

The green marble columns were taken from the Artemis Temple of Ephesus which was known as one of the Seven Wonders of the World, and the porphyritic columns of Baalbek were erected in the main hall.

The inauguration of the church was so pompous, that even the emperor could not refrain from shouting, "Oh, Solomon, I have outdone you!" upon seeing the splendour inside.

The Architecture

St. Sophia, which is the unsurpassable example of Byzantine art, is evaluated to be the synthesis of eastern and western architectural traditions. The basilican church plan with three naves, which was known since early times, was united with the central plan in St. Sophia and a huge dome came to cover the central hall.

The church which is dated back to the early period of Byzantine art was built under Roman influence. As Byzantine art inclined more towards eastern art in the following periods, St. Sophia came to be the only monument in her unique style and one of the most outstanding monuments of world art in general.

The inner space of St. Sophia is composed of the inner and outer narthexes, a central nave covered by the central dome, two smaller side narthexes and a gallery which can be reached from the inner narthex.

Alterations and Restorations

The first cracks in the dome became visible after the earthquakes of 553 and 557, and a large part of the dome collapsed in 558. The second dome was smaller than the first one but it was seven meters higher; and it was constructed with special bricks made of tufa, so that the dome would be lighter. The tufa bricks were brought in from Rhodes.

The inner decorations of the church were changed during the Iconoclastic Period (726-842 A.D): The icons and all the panels ornamented with figures were put away with and were replaced by simple crosses representing Jesus Christ and Virgin Mary.

The western part of the building was damaged again by an earthquake in 869 and restored in 870.

A part of the central dome was demolished by another earthquake on 25 October 986 and was restored by architect Tridot. St. Sophia was plundered and partly destroyed by the crusaders of the Fourth Crusade in 1204.

Restoration of the church began in 1261 when the city was taken back from the crusaders. Supporting pillars were added to its western sections, and Andranicos II had still other pillars added to its north- eastern and south- western sections.

The dome, which had collapsed during the earthquake in 1348, was restored in 1354 with the special tax collected from the city dwellers.

The Ottoman Era

The Turks converted the building into a mosque after they seized and took the city on 29 May 1453.

The first wooden minaret and the "mihrab" indicating the direction of Mecca were built during the reign of Mehmet II. None of these constructions has reached our day. The brick minaret at the south-east of the building was built during the reign of Mehmet the Conqueror.

Mimar Sinan is the architect of the minaret at the north-east which was built under Selim II (1566-1574). The other two minarets at the north-west and at the south-west were added in the time of Murat III (1574-1595).

A sultan's mausoleum was built in the garden during the reign of Selim II. Other additional elements were, an Imam's gallery out of marble, a preacher's lectern and a tiled sultan's gallery which was altered during

Fossati's restoration later on.

A library was built inside (1736) and an elementary school outside (1742) the building during the reign of Mahmut I.

Restoration work was done again under Mahmut II in 1810 but the most important restoration was done by the Swiss architect G. Fossati in 1847-49 during Sultan Abdülmecid's rule (1839- 1861). The sultan's gallery was added in this period.

The Decorations:

We know that the interior of the building had various decorations when the church was finished in the sixth century. But we are not certain whether figurative mosaics were among them or not. It is generally accepted, that the geometric and the floral decorations inside are left from that period.

If there were any scenes with human figures, they must have been demolished during the Iconoclastic Period (728-842). All the figures we see now are dated back to the period after 842. Because Islam forbids figures in places of worship, only the faces of the human figures in St. Sophia were covered up first but then they were all painted towards the middle of the 18th century.

Most of these figures were brought into daylight by the American Byzantine Institute starting with 1932. The mosaics seen in St. Sophia are scenes dedicated to specific persons and made throughout the centuries. The classical scenes in church interiors which tell of the lives of Jesus Christ and Virgin Mary are not seen in Byzantine art. And there is no coherence of style in St. Sophia's figurative panels.

The Tour Plan of St. Sophia

The entrance is at the west side through the garden. After the mosque was converted into a museum in 1935, many pieces have been

*The central hall, a view
from the south-eastern section.*

St. Sophia, entrance from the outer narthex.

Ruins of St. Sophia from the era of Theodosius II.

The mosaic over the Imperial Portal, Emperor Leon VI. asks Jesus for matrimonial permission.

collected in the garden to be preserved and exhibited. Such elements are not directly connected to the building.

You can see the ruins of the former St. Sophia of the era of Theodosius II in the ditch before you enter St. Sophia from the portal at the west.

You pass through the inner and outer narthexes before you step into the main building. The outer narthex is 5.75 m wide and has a simple structure. The stucco tablets where the decisions of the Council of 1116 are written are to be seen in this section. There are five doors which lead to the inner narthex. The mosaics which were discovered during the restoration of Guillaume Fossati in the era of Sultan Abdülmecid are at the left side of the door at the center. These mosaics show Abdülmecid's imperial signature made by the Italian master Lanzoni.

The Inner Narthex

The inner narthex is wider and higher than the outer one. The ceiling is decorated with geometrically designed mosaics on a golden basis and the walls are covered with thinly veined marble plates. Both sides of the inner narthex lead to the slopes that wind up to the gallery.

There is also a side entrance called the Horologion Door at the south. This entrance which has the form of a room was sometimes used as the emperor's entrance door at some ceremonies.

The central door at the inner narthex which leads to the central hall is called the Imperial Door. The emperor used to kneel down here before he entered the central hall of the church. In the mosaic above this door, we see Jesus Christ sitting on the preciously

St. Sophia, a general view of the central hall.

St. Sophia, views from the central hall.

A view of the central hall.

The mosaic of St. Ignatius.

ornamented throne at the center, holding an inscript which reads, "May peace fall on you all.

I am the light of the world", Gabriel in the medallion on the right, and Virgin Mary on the left.

It is usually believed, that the figure kneeling at the left is Emperor Leon VI who begs Christ for permission for a new marriage.

Emperor Leon VI has married three times though this was against Orthodox rules, never had a son by his wives but had one by his mistress, Zoe, and begged Christ to allow him to marry her and make her the mother of his future sons.

This mosaic was made in 920, covered up by the Ottomans, and disposed again after the restoration in 1933.

The Main Hall

After we enter the main hall from the Imperial Door, we see that the marble floor near the door has sunk a little due to the constant guard of soldiers in Byzantine times.

The inner length of the main hall is 73.50 meters and its width is 69.50 meters. The apsis is at its eastern walls. The central nave is distinguished from the side naves through four big columns and supports. The central dome is 55.60 meters high and its diameter is between 31.24 and 32.81 meters because it is not an

The mosaic of Emperor Alexander.

The mosaic of Virgin Mary and the Child on the semi-dome of the absis.

even circle. The dome, which was more flat at the time of construction, was damaged by the earthquake in 558, was restored afterwards and rebuilt with windows and pendants. Light bricks brought in from Rhodes were used for the reconstruction.

There is a Quran verse written by Kazasker Mustafa İzzet at the center of the dome. It is believed, that a picture of Christ the Savior has stood at the center during the Byzantine Empire.

Cherubs are painted in the four pendants under the dome.

Their faces were covered up with golden medaillons during the restorations in the 19th century because Islam forbids figures in places of worship.

The four round panels with a diameter of 7.5 meters each, which are as high as the gallery, were constructed by Kazasker Mustafa İzzet during the reign of Sultan Abdülmecid in the 19th century, and bear the names of God, Prophet Muhammed, the four caliphs; Abubakr, Omar, Othman and Ali, and the names of Ali's sons, Hasan and Hüseyin.

There are crosses on the marble floor in the main hall. They are at specific intervals along the circumference of the dome.

The columns erected in the church were taken from different temples within the

boundaries of the empire. The green marble columns in the main hall were brought from the Temple of Artemis in Ephesus and the porphyric ones from Baalbek.

There are 107 columns in St. Sophia, 47 of which are in the ground floor and 60 are in the upper one.

The monograms of Emperor Justinianus and his wife Theodora can be seen at the centers of the capitals.

The large marble jars and vases of the Hellenistic period seen at the two sides of the entrance are approximately three tons heavy and were brought from Pergamum.

They were placed in St. Sophia during the reign of Murat III (1574-1595), and were

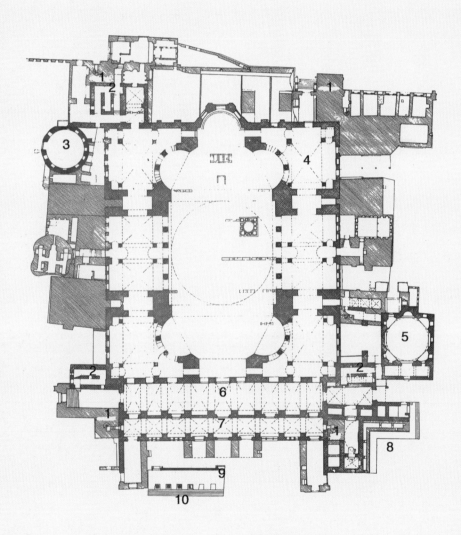

St. Sophia, the plan of the first floor.

1- Minaret

2- Staircase

3- Skevophylakion

4- Metatorium

5- Baptistery

6- Narthex

7- Vestibule

8- Remnants of the Patriarcal Palace

9- Remnants of the Atrium

10- Theodosian Vestibule

An inner view of the library built during the reign of Mahmud I.

A view of the Sultan's niche.

St. Sophia, an inner view.

probably used for the ritual washings before prayer.

The central space, which is decorated with colorful mosaics, is accepted to be the place of the crowning ceremony of the new emperor, and is thought to be built in a later age.

The figure of Virgin Mary holding the Child is seen on the golden base of the half-dome of the apsis.

This is the first figured panel made after the Iconoclastic Period. There is some evidence to date it back to the era before 867. Besides the eternally beautiful Virgin Mary holding Christ in this section, there are two archangel figures facing each other at the lower ends of the big arch here.

Only the feet of one of the angels can be seen at the left today but the other figure is in a much better condition. This second figure is accepted to be Gabriel, and this mosaic is as

old as the one with Virgin Mary.

We see the Imam's pew built in the 16th century at the right as we walk towards the apsis.

The mosque niche which shows the direction of Mecca was built after the church was turned to a mosque in the 15th century. Architect G. Fossati has built the gallery of the sultan during Abdülmecid's rule in the 19th century.

The library built by Sultan Mahmut I in 1736 is to be seen in the southern nave. This construction is a beautiful example of Turkish art with its cupboard doors inlaid with mother-of-pearl, Koran stands and tiles.

There is a column called the "perspiring column" to the south-west of of the northern nave.

There are quite a number of myths about this column. Today, people stick their fingers

Gallery, the marble doon at the southern end.　　*The decorated columns of the galleries.*

in a hole on the column as they murmur their wishes.

The Galleries

The galleries which we reach over the slopes in the north and in the south used to be the ladies' departments. In the beginning, men and women used to pay religious service separately.

This section with a cradle vault which extends over the whole side naves and narthex has the empress' seat right at the center across the apsis.

This place is separated by the thin mosaic strips on the floor and has joists with wooden ornaments which art historians favor very much. There is a section at the southern end of the gallery, separated by a marble portal and rich with mosaic panes, which was called

the Priests' Rooms in the Ottoman era. The marble section at the center is popularly known as the door to heaven and hell. The ceremonial book written by Emperor Constantine Porphyrogenitus (913-959) indicates, that this section was used at those ceremonies which the emperor and the patriarch attended.

A high quality mosaic pane attracts attention right after this portal. The picture here is called the Deisis scene and shows Christ at the center with Virgin Mary at his right and John the Baptist at his left. The bottom part of the pane with a golden background has been demolished.

This pane is the most outstanding one in the whole church when style and quality are concerned.

In this picture, Virgin Mary and John the Baptist are shown begging Christ for mercy for mankind at the Doomsday. Christ must be sitting on a throne which is now extinct with only a part of the stool under his foot. He blesses with one hand and holds the Bible with the other. There is a deep sorrow marked on the faces of all the figures.

The emperor mosaics at the two sides of the southern window of the upper gallery are crucial because they are true portraits of the persons they display.

Among these panes, the mosaic in the north of the southern gallery shows Christ in the middle with Emperor Constantine Monomachus (1042-1055) at his left and Empress Zoe (1028-1050) at his right.

Empress Zoe married a number of times, and the picture and the name of the emperor on the pane were changed everytime she had a new spouse.

She was married either to her first husband, Romanus III Argyrus or her second husband, Michael IV Paphlagonian when the first painting was made. The mosaic shows Empress Zoe and her third husband, Constantine IX Monomachus, in rich ceremonial arrays decorated with precious gem stones.

The emperor offers a pouch of gold to Jesus Christ sitting on the throne at the center. An inscript reading, "Constantine Monomachus, the Emperor of the Romans" is seen on the emperor's figure.

The empress is shown holding a paper roll which legalizes the emperor's donation. Christ is shown in a simple navy blue gown, and he sits on an ornamented throne, holding a pane with a cross in one hand and blessing them with the other. This mosaic dates back to the XI. century.

The mosaic near it shows Emperor John II Comnenus (1118-1143) offering a pouch of money to Virgin Mary who holds the Child on her lap. Empress Eirene, who was the daughter of the Hungarian king, is shown near him and she is holding a paper roll which legalizes his donation. Their son Alexius, who

St. Sophia, the mosaic of Deisis.

The mosaic of Deisis with Virgin Mary, Jesus Christ and St. John the Baptist.

died of pneumonia (1112), is pictured on the side wall. The whole family is dressed in rich ceremonial clothing.

The emperor, his blond and rosy-cheeked spouse and their sick son are all given with realistic details. This mosaic dates back to the XII. century.

The picture of Alexander, the brother of Leon VI, is seen at a corner in the northern gallery. The reason for Alexander to be shown in such a dark corner is not clear especially when we consider his co-regency with his brother.

This mosaic dates back to 912-913. The mosaics of prominent clergymen are seen in the huge vaults covering the side naves. These

clergymen are Ignatios the younger, the Patriarch of İstanbul, John Chrysostomos, and the Patriarch of Antioch, Ignatios Theophorus.

The Exit

Over the door to the south of the inner narthex, we see Virgin Mary with Child at the center, Emperor Justinian at her right and Emperor Constantine at her left. This entrance was used by some emperors who attended the ceremonies in St. Sophia.

The emperor portraits which were added to the pane during the reign of Basil II (976-1025) and excavated in 1933 are not genuine portraits: One of the emperors displayed here

The gallery in the XIX. century (the Fosatti Collection).

lived in the IV. and the other in the VI. centuries but both of them are shown in the ceremonial dresses of the X. century. Emperor Justinian to the right of Virgin Mary is holding a model of St. Sophia of which he was the founder, and his name and attributes are written beside it. Both emperors are shown wearing golden gowns and with crowns on their heads.

Virgin Mary sits on a throne at the center with the Child on her lap. Jesus holds a paper roll denoting his deity and blesses with his other hand. The word "Theodokes" (mother of God) in abbreviated form is seen on both sides of Mary's head.

There is a bronze door in this section which was brought in from a Hellenistic temple in Tarsus.

The door dates back to the II. century B.C and the ornaments on it are worthy of

attraction. It was placed in St. Sophia during the reign of Theophilus (829-842) in the Iconoclastic Period. This door is the present exit of the museum.

The Sultans' Tombs
The Tomb of Selim II

Sinan is the architect of this tomb which was built in 1577. This square mausoleum has two domes and is coated with marble on the outside. It is decorated with outstanding tiles inside.

Sultan Selim II, Nurbanu Sultan, Gevher Sultan, Selim II's son Abdullah, and some of his other sons and daughters are buried in the mausoleum.

Emperors' mosaics in the southern gallery.

Mozaik XII. asır
İmparator Ioannes II.Komnenos
İmparatoriçe İren ve Alexios
Ortada Meryem kucağında İsa.

Mozaik XII.Century
Emperor John II.Komnenos
Empress Irene and their son Alexios
in the center Virgin Mary and child.

Mozaik XI. Asır
İmparator Konstantin Monamakos
İsa ve imparatorice Zoe.

Mozaik XI. Century
Emperor Constantin IX.Monomachos
Christ and empress zoe.

Jesus Christ, with Emperor Constantine IX Monomachus on the left and Empress Zoë on the right.

Virgin Mary and the Christ-Child, Emperor Camnenos II and Empress Irene.

Mosaic with Emperor Justinian, Virgin Mary and the Child where Constantin offers the model of St. Sophia.

The Mausoleum of Murat III

This mausoleum was built by architect Davut Ağa and completed after the sultan's death. It has a hexagonal plan and the mausoleum is covered with marble plates and coral red tiles in the XVI. century. Murat III's mother, Safiye Sultan, his sons and his daughters are also buried here.

The Mausoleum of Mehmet III

This octagonal mausoleum is the work of architect Dalgıç Ahmet. It is covered with marble plates on the outside. İznik tiles decorate the inner walls. Sultan Mehmet III,

A general view of the mosaic over the exit.

Fountain at the exit of St. Sophia.

The mausoleum of Sultan Murad III.

Ahmet III's mother, Handan Sultan, the sons and daughters of Ahmet I, and Murat III's daughter, Ayşe Sultan, are buried here.

The Tomb of Sultan İbrahim and Mustafa I

St. Sophia's baptism hall was used as an oil mill for a short period after the conquest. When Mustafa I died in 1623, a proper place could not be found, and the oil mill was turned into a mausoleum.

Sultan İbrahim was buried in the same place when he died in 1648. This mausoleum has no decorations other than an engraving done with a pen.

Inner view of Murad III's mausoleum.

The St. Sophia Fountain

Sultan Mahmud I (1730-1754) favored the foundations of Ayasofya very much and had an elementary school, a clock room and the Ayasofya Fountain built in the garden. The Fountain is fully in the style of the Tulip Era and one of the best examples of Turkish art. This Fountain has eight marble columns and its lead eaves rest on eight wide arches. The monumental fountain's inscription tells us, that it was built in 1740.

Tile Panel at the mausoleum of Murad III.

The Yerebatan Cistern

The Yerebatan Cistern (Basilica Cistern) is one of the most eloquent monuments left from the Byzantine Empire.

It was ordered by Emperor Justinian in the VI. century. It covers a very big area of 9800 square meters, and is 70 meters wide and 140 meters long. Its water storing capacity is 80 000 cubic meters.

Its thick walls and floor covering enable water to be stored without any loss.The roof of the cistern, which has cross-shaped vaults and circular bindings, rests on eight-meter-long columns.

The 336 columns in the cistern are either made of marble or granite and Corinthian or Doric. Some are composed of two pieces; whereas some are a single piece. Most of the columns are cylindrical, and the most interesting one is the one with tear drop designs on it.

Two of the columns are set on pedestals with Medusa heads on them. One of the Medusa heads is upside down and the other is put sideways.

The idea behind such a positioning and the source of the stone blocks are unknown. There are two interpretations:

- These two pedestals were used to have the corresponding columns as high as the rest of the columns in the cistern.

- They were placed in the cistern to protect it from the evil eye.

According to Greek mythology, Medusa is one of the three Gorgons of the underworld (Hades) and has the power to turn anyone into stone who dares to look at her. Thus, Medusa heads have been used in the buildings constructed in antiquity for protection and to avert the evil spirits.

The Yerebatan Cistern.

The Yerebatan Cistern was built to supply water to the Byzantine palace and to the buildings around it. Ottomans have also used it for a long time.

The cistern was supplied with water which was brought from the Belgrade Forests 19 kilometers away and transported over viaducts.

There used to be a big church in its place in the early Roman Age where legal matters were also settled. It was destroyed in a fire in

covered with cement during these restorations and have thus lost their original state.

The cistern was turned into a museum after the foundation of the Turkish Republic and sightseeing in boats was introduced.

The final restoration started in 1985 and tons of earth and mud were excavated. The water level is low ever since and the platform on it enables the visitors to reach the farthest corners.

Yerebatan Cistern; Medusa heads used as column pedestals.

476 but rebuilt by Emperor Iulius later on.

It was demolished in a second fire after the Nika Revolt and restored by Emperor Justinian.

The underground cistern has been occasionally restored since its time of construction. Two of the restorations under the Ottomans were first by architect Mehmet Ağa of Kayseri during the reign of Ahmet III in the 18th century, and seconly under Abdülhamit II in the 19th century. Some of the columns were

The restoration was completed in 1987 and visitors can now cherish its beauty accompanied by music and light beams.

The Chora Church
Kariye Museum

The Chora Church.

We do not have much knowledge on the church of the Chora Monastery, which was dedicated to Jesus Christ, but the existence of a very old religious complex here is generally accepted due to the old Greek word "Chora" which means "suburb".

If we regard the Constantine Walls to be the city limits, this church lay on the outskirts of the town and was integrated to the inner city with the city walls built in the 5th century.

The Kariye Museum.

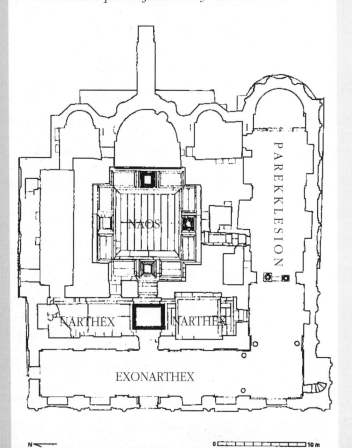

The plan of the Kariye Museum.

PAREKKLESION

NAOS

NARTHEX   NARTHEX

EXONARTHEX

N

0 [_____] 10 m

This church existed as it is until the Comnenian dynasty but then began to be used as a chapel of the Blakhernai Palace when the latter became the center of political rule. The Chora Monastery stood in ruins towards the end of the XI. century and was restored by Maria Dukina, the mother-in-law of Alexius Comnenus I (1081-1118), and dedicated to Christ the Savior. Then, it was demolished again and restored by the younger son of Alexius I, Isaac, who had a magnificent grave built for himself in the narthex section of the church. That mausoleum was brought to another monastery in Thrace later on. The Chora Monastery was destroyed like all the other buildings of the city during the Latin invasion dating back to 1204-1261.

The Chora Monastery was rebuilt and redecorated with mosaics and frescos by Theodorus Metokides after the Latin

The Chora Museum, general view from the Naos.

invasion. This restoration dating back to 1303-1328 was the final one which gave the church its present look. Metokides was one of the outstanding intellectuals of the so-called Last Byzantine Era between 1261 and 1453 which was the year of the Turkish conquest. He was expelled from duty during the reign of Andronicus II (1282-1328) and spent the rest of his life as a simple monk in the Chora Monastery. The building gained importance during the Turkish siege, and the famous Icon of Virgin Mary, which was believed to protect the city and had been preserved in the Church of Hodegetria in Sarayburnu, was carried to Chora because the building was close to the city-walls. After the Turkish conquest, the church remained deserted for a time, and was turned into a mosque by Beyazıd II's grand vizier, Atik Ali Pasha, in 1511. From then on, it came to be called the Chora mosque. It

became a museum in 1948 and its frescos were cleaned and restored by the American Byzantine Institute.

Nothing is left from the Chora Monastery other than the church. The oldest part of the church built in the XI.-XII. centuries is composed of a single narthex and a central hall which were set on the foundations of an older building. The central hall is covered with a big cupola with a high drum which sits on four vaults that are carried by massive corner supports. The central hall has a Kiborion plan. There are cells (prothesis, diakonikon) covered by smaller cupolas at both sides of a protruding apsis. The southern section at the far right of the inner narthex is accepted to be the burial place which Isaac Comnenus had once prepared for himself. This section is covered by a windowed cupola with a high drum.

Mosaic of Virgin Mary at the Naos.

General view of the Paraklession.

Theodorus Metokides has built a supplementary chapel with a single nave at the south side of the main building during the first years of the XIV. century. This long and narrow place, called the Pareklession, rests on a cellar in the same form. There is a windowed cupola with a high dome at the center of this section which is actually a mausoleum chapel. This place is attached to a corridor which extends along the west front and makes up the outer narthex. The front of this L-shaped supplementary building, which enfolds the central building, is a lively one where typical Byzantine stone and brick work of the later periods attracts attention.

The attributes of the Chora mosaics and frescos can be described in the following manner: The bodies in the pictures are made in the one to nine ratio like sculptor Lisipos has done in antiquity, that is the body is nine times longer than the head, which renders a long and elegant figure. The angry look used on the faces throughout the Dark Ages lacks here, and the Jesus figures are warmer and more human. All the figures look stable and are placed according to basic perspective rules. Paintings, rocks and architectural designs seen in the background make the pictures three-dimensional. The scenes are made with special care for them to look daily, lively and ordinary. The figures are voluminous due to the folds in their costumes and their gestures. Designs like allegorical figures or cloth pieces painted on roofs which were frequently used in antiquity are also to be cherished here. Lots of plant figures and geometric shapes also help to break any monotony in the pictures. The scenes are enriched with explicating stories near them. The main composition in the mausoleum chapel (paraklesion) is the

The outer narthex; Mary and Joseph on the way to Betlehem.

Doomsday, and the lives of Mary and Christ are told in detail in the inner and outer narthexes. Visitors are advised to start at the inner narthex in order not to miss the chronology of the events.

The Mosaics of the Outer Narthex

The scenes telling of Jesus Christ's childhood and life are to be seen in a chronological order starting at the north wing. The source for these scenes are the canonic bibles. Although there is some damage, these scenes are usually well-preserved. The decorative paintings and apostle portraits among the scenes enrich the total look further.

Joseph's Dream
Joseph is leaning on his arm in this scene, and he gets the newsin his dream, that Mary has conceived a child by the Holy Spirit, and that Christ is to be born. An angel descending from the heavens whispers in his ear. In the background, we see Mary and her two friends in a spot somewhere outside of town.

The Journey to Betlehem
In the scene, which is at the right of the same vault, we see Joseph, Mary and one of Joseph's sons going to Betlehem for a census, Betlehem being Joseph's birth place.

The Census Made For Collecting Tax
In this picture, we see Joseph and his family before Quirinius, the governor of Syria, and his other sons are also in the scene beside Virgin Mary. Joseph presents Mary and the clerk takes notice of all their names. The governor on a throne and Mary are longer than the rest of the people. This method is

Mary's and Joseph's family before Quirinius, the Mayor of Syria.

frequently observed in Byzantine art when persons of importance are to be underlined. The backgrounds of both Mary and the governor are the same which makes them symmetrical figures.

The Birth of Christ

The scene we see at the center of the eastern vault is a rather crowded composition. Mary is observed half- sitting on a piece of red cloth at the center with baby Christ in a cradle at her side. The beam of light falling on the cradle symbolizes God, and the cow and the donkey near the cradle are there to warm up the cave. Joseph sits outside the cave and ponders while two midwives wash the baby. We see two groups of shepherds and angels behind Mary. Three shepherds of various ages at the right are faced with the happy news of Christ's birth and look bewildered. One of the

angels extends his hand to them and his words are written in three lines at his side. The other angels behind Mary's head converse with each other.

Three Soothsayers Entering the Presence of King Herod

This scene, which is placed at the southern wing of the outer narthex, is composed of two consecutive pictures. In the first one, we see the three soothsayers of various ages on their horses.

They have followed a star to be there. In the second picture, thay are shown before King Herod. The old soothsayer presents his gifts to him.

Herod's Investigation

We see King Herod on his throne and a guard in this scene the half of which has been

Mosaic on the birth and the first bath of Jesus.

ruined. When Herod hears of another king's birth, he asks the priests and the soothsayers for information.

The Massacre of the Innocent Ones

Although a large area was devoted to this scene, most of it has been destroyed. This scene follows at the end of the southern wing and over the window on the western wall. King Herod orders the massacre of all the children below the age of two after he has talked to the soothsayers. We see Herod with soldiers in front of him at the left, and a soldier who has killed a baby and the baby's mother at the right. We see a group of weeping and mourning mothers in the scene over the window.

Elizabeth Running Away With John

Elizabeth runs away with her child, John the Baptist, and seeks refuge in a cave in the scene on the western vault over the window. The soldiers following them cannot enter the cave because a miracle has happened and the cave opening has been blocked by rocks.

The Holy Family Returns From Egypt

In the first part of this scene, we see Joseph dreaming of an angel who tells him to return from Egypt to Nazareth. The family is on the way in the second part of the scene. Bare-footed Joseph carries Jesus on his shoulder, Mary and one of Joseph's sons follow him,

Three eastern soothsayers before King Herod.

and the city seen from afar must be Nazareth.

Jesus Goes to Jerusalem on Easter

This is the last scene concerning the childhood of Jesus. Joseph, the twelve-year-old Jesus, Mary and Joseph's sons are pictured going to Jerusalem in the scene which is painted in the last arch of the western wall.

Jesus and John the Baptist Meet Each Other

The scene takes place at the banks of the Jordan River. John the Baptist is wrapped up in sheep skin and is pointing at Jesus.

Satan's Trial of Jesus

Satan's trial of Jesus is seen at the south of the arch vault. Satan appears before Jesus, who has stayed forty days long at the desert after his baptism, and wants to test him but Jesus refuses him every time he wants to. In the first scene, they are seen in front of a chest filled with stones. Satan asks Jesus to turn the stones into bread and offers him all the kingdoms of the earth. Six richly dressed figures are seen here whom Satan offers to Jesus with a gesture of his hand. In another trial, he takes Jesus to the top of a high building and tells him to fly. Satan is shown as a little black figure with wings in all of these scenes.

The Wonders of the Canaan Wedding

Some of the parts of the scene, which is on the arch vault of the entrance, have been ruined, and only the pendant designs at the

Detail from the massacre of the innocent.

lower section can be seen. Servants who fill water into jugs of baked earth, and Jesus and Mary, who walk towards an older figure offering water to Christ, can be observed.

Increasing the Bread

In the other pendant, Christ is seen in front of three full bread baskets. He extends bread to two of his apostles. A crowd of people stand waiting in the background.

The fresco, Christ the Savior, is observed right across the entrance door.

Christ the Savior

This is a unique composition of Byzantine art. This picture displays Christ as the embodiment of both the father and the holy son. Christ sitting on a throne is a prominent figure in western art whereby his creating and healing abilities are emphasized. Christ has always been drawn as a bust in Byzantine art and placed either on apsides or in the domes which stood for the skies, that is, the house of God.

Jesus Christ is usually seen holding the Holy Bible in his right hand and blessing with the other. Christ the Savior faces the entrance in the Chora Church as if he welcomes the visitors. The left side of the picture is wider and he therefore looks as if he has turned sideways a little bit. Considering the shades of color on his face, this picture is certainly not a monotonous one. Artists used to work in a more independent style during the last phases of the Byzantine Empire.

The Mosaics of the Inner Narthex

Virgin Mary's childhood and life are pictured in detail in the northern wing of the inner narthex. The chronological order of the mosaics make them look like a film roll. There

The wonders of Jesus:
Water turns to wine.

is no information about Mary's childhood and family in the Bible, and such details have always attracted the attention of the masses throughout the ages. Detailed information on these themes can be found in the "Protevangile de Jacques", "L'Evangile du Pseudo-Matthieu", and "L'Evangile de la nativité de la Vierge".

Joachim's Offering Gets Refused

In the scene placed in the western pendant of the northern cupola, we observe four pillars representing a temple. Bearded Zacharias with long white hair is seen under the dome. The doors of the temple are closed and he gesticulates a refusing sign. Joachim's offerings to the temple have not been accepted. The mosaics of the following section have been ruined.

Mosaic of Christ the Savor with detail over the entrance of the Naos.

From the mosaics of the inner narthex: Mary's birth.

Joachim Among the Shepherds

This scene is right across the one above. Here we see two sad and pondering shepherds talking and walking towards Joachim.

Communicating Good News to Anna

Gabriel descends from the heavens in the scene in the vault over the eastern wall and communicates the good news to Anna, who stands beside a pool in a garden. Anna extends both hands to the angel and talks to him. The waters of the pool symbolize Anna's childless youth.

Hugging Before the Golden Door

An aged couple hug each other in the picture made in a narrow space. The background shows the door to Jerusalem.

The Birth of Mary

The scene painted on the vault of the second section on the eastern wall is pretty crowded. Anna lies on the bed after delivery in the front, and newly born Mary is being washed in the lower section at the right. One of the midwives fills the tub with water and the other holds the baby. Mary is pictured healthy and naked. Women accosting Anna present her with gifts, and a servant at her feet waves a feathered fan to make a little breeze. Joachim is seen in an edifice at the right, and he looks in the room hesitantly. His bashfulness is stamped on his face.

The First Seven Steps of Mary

In this composition, Mary walks towards her mother with slow steps. The servant behind her extends her arms towards the child and is in a slightly bending position. She is pictured as if she is ready to hold the child in case she stumbles.

Mosaic on Mary's first seven steps.

Mary is Being Loved by Her Family

This picture is over the birth scene inside the vault. Mary's parents are in a sitting position, and they hug Mary lovingly. The peacock figure at the side is an allegorical sign which shows tha family's joy.

Priests Sanctify Mary

In the scene painted on the western part of the vault, Joachim holds Mary in his arms, and walks towards three priests who are seated at a table. They invite Joachim whose profile can be seen.

Introduction to the Temple and Mary Being Fed by the Angel

Two different scenes are interwoven here: Three-year-old Mary is taken to the temple by her family and is dedicated to God. She walks steadily towards Zacharias who is ready to greet her. She climbs up the steps without any help from her family and reaches the temple as she displays a determination unexpected of her age. Mary is under the dome which rests on four pillars in the second picture. Here she takes the food the priests give her and distributes it to the poor because she is fed by angels herself.

Mary Takes the Ball of Wool

In the scene which we observe on the outer door of the inner narthex, Mary takes a violet ball of wool in order to cover up the temple with a piece of cloth. Mary, who has been chosen from among the other girls in the temple, stands right before three priests sitting at the center and takes the ball of wool from the farthest one. The girls in the group are older than Mary, and they converse with an expression of jealousy stamped on their faces.

Virgin Mary being loved by her family.

The Prayer of Zacharias

Zacharias is to marry Mary with a widower as he has been informed by an angel. He asks all the widowed and unmarried men to bring a twig to the temple. Mary is pictured here under a dome and among four pillars which represent the temple, and twigs have been lined up on the table before her. Zacharias kneels down and looks as if he is at prayer.

Joseph Gets Chosen

In the scene which we see at the center of the western wall, the priest is holding a green twig and his other hand is on Mary's head. Joseph is among the group facing them, and he takes a step forward.

Joseph Takes Mary to His Home

In this scene on the vault, Joseph is with Mary and his son. She is following Joseph and the boy who have turned their heads towards her. Joseph shows her the way with his hand.

Chalk for Mary

In the scene which we observe in the western pendants of the northern cupola, Mary is near the well and looks startled at the voice of the angel. She holds a pitcher. Archangel Gabriel is at the right.

Joseph Takes Leave of Mary

Joseph bids farewell because he takes his son and goes to a distant place to work. We see carpenter's tools in the basket which is at the boy's back. Visitors should go to the northern wing of the outer narthex after these scenes which tell of Mary's life.

Virgin Mary being sanctifed by the priests.

The Mosaics at the Southern Wing of the Inner Narthex

We see Jesus healing sick people in a group of mosaics which are at the southern section. One of Christ's attributes is his healing power; therefore, sick people are given deep attention here.

Healing a Bedridden Person in Carpharnaum

Christ accosts a paralyzed person lying on a bed in the left side of the eastern pendant. He holds a roll as he does in all the miracle scenes. He has healed the sick person with his other hand without touching him. One of the apostles who are at the side of the bed looks at Christ in awe.

Healing a Woman Who Suffers From Loss of Blood

In the scene which is at the right of the eastern pendant, a woman who has been suffering from loss of blood, throws herself at his feet in order to touch his clothes as Christ is on the way to Jairos' house.

Healing a Person Sick With Lepra and Another One With a Dried up Hand

In the scenes which are over the vault leading to the paraklession, a leper and a person whose arm is sick, are pictured begging Christ for health. The leper is half-naked and has red spots all over his body, and the other ill person extends his arm forward.

Healing the Blind and the Deaf

A blind and a deaf person are seen at the left of the western pendant and two blind people at the right. Christ walks towards the blind people who sit under a tree before the walls of Jericho and sanctifies them.

Mary takes the ball of wool from the priest.

Healing a Lot of Sick People

This is a crowded composition covering the whole vault. Christ walks towards a group of sick people and he is followed by his apostles. The most important figure in the group is the woman who reaches out a child to Christ. The illness in the child's legs is obvious. Some of the other sick people are pictured sitting in front of that woman and some are in a standing position behind her.

There are independent scenes from Mary's and Christ's lives in the inner narthex. In the large mosaic which fills up the first vault at the northern wing, "Christ of Khalke and Mary" are pictured. Art historians interpret this scene in various ways. Some of them date it back to the XII. century when Isaac Comnenus had a thorough restoration made in the church. Isaac's picture near Mary's is the reason for this interpretation. This mosaic bears that

name because it looks like a Christ icon which decorates the portal of the imperial palace in Constantinople. Virgin Mary is at the right and is pictured begging for intercession. The priestess at the bottom is Maria Paleologus who lived in the XIV. century. The inscription beside the figure reads, "Melane, the lady of the Mongols". Both of these persons must have been pictured here because they have protected the monastery though at different ages.

Christ and Methokides

Christ is sitting on a rich and jewelled throne in the scene which is over the entrance door opening to the central hall. He holds a Bible in one hand and sanctifies with the other. Theodorus Methokides kneels down before him holding a model of the church. He was the controller of the Treasury and his title

Jesus heals a lot of sick people.

A sick woman who wants to touch Jesus' frock.

Panel with Mary and Christ at the inner narthex.

General view over the entrance of the Naos.

is written beside his figure. He is pictured in an array which looks like a caftan and a turban.

In the mosaics at the sides of the main entrance, we see St. Paul and St. Peter. St. Peter is holding the key of heaven and St. Paul is holding the holy book in his left hand. St. Paul is one of the most successful mosaics with regard to facial expression.

The Cupolas of the Inner Narthex

The scenes in the cupolas of the inner narthex show Christ's whole lineage. Christ the Savior is seen in the pendant which is at the center of the southern cupola. In the binding areas among the cupola sections, twenty-four figures beginning with Adam and ending with Jacob are pictured.

There are fifteen other figures lined up in the lower row. The mother of God, "Maria Theodokos" is pictured with Child at the center of the northern dome. Other persons of her pedigree are lined up in two rows around her.

The Central Hall

This old part of the church which dates back to the XI. century is square shaped. A mosque niche, which always shows the direction of Mecca, has been added to the protruding apsis in the Turkish age. Only a few mosaics of this section have reached our day. The Christ and Mary panes at both sides of the apsis were revealed as late as 1956. Foreign travelers' notes tell us, that these mosaics were either covered with stucco or hid under wooden panes when the church served as a mosque in the Turkish era.

The Mosaic of Jesus Christ

In this partly ruined mosaic, we observe Christ in a standing position with an open book in his left hand and sanctifying with the right one. The inscription in the open book reads: "Ye, exhausted people and all of you under a heavy burden, come to me, I will give you peace".

Mary Hodigitria

Byzantine art has favored Mary as "Hodigitria" very much. The word comes from the Greek origin of "hodos", meaning, "one who shows the way". The source of this attribute is an icon which Christianity has accepted to be made by Luke as Mary stood model to him, and which is in a church in İstanbul.

Koimesis

Byzantine art calls the scene of Mary's death "Koimesis" denoting "the sleep of death". In Mary's

General view of the Naos.

death scenes, Christ, who has died long before his mother, descends to the world and takes his mother's soul up to the heavens. Christ is shown in a white halo, which is the symbol of his descent, and with a cherub behind his head, which is the guard of his heavenly throne. The child in his arms symbolizes Mary's soul, and his hands are covered with a cloth, denoting the respect he has for his mother. Mary lying on a bed constitutes the lower part of the triangular composition, and a crowd composed of apostles, priests and women is distributed evenly in the picture. The figure holding a censer at the head of the bed is St. Pierre. Paul, Luke, Mark and Andrew are at the foot of the bed.

Paraklesion Anastis

This scene which is on one of the twelve Christian feasts covers the semi-dome of the apsis. After Jesus was crucified, his mortal body died but then he was reborn. He descended to the underworld and sanctified the souls who had lived before him and were not baptized before he ascended to the heavens and the seat of God. But before he descended to the underworld, he sent John the Baptist there to inform the underworld, that he was to come. Hades, thereupon, ordered the satans to close the doors and fortify the locks. But all the doors shattered and the underworld was lit when Christ arrived there. That very moment is the theme of the mosaic here. Broken and shattered locks and door pieces can be observed under Christ's feet who arrives in Hades in his floating robe. The underworld or hell, as it is called in Byzantine art, is the place where the dead await the last judgement and the Doomsday. This place is also called "Limbe" and is ruled by the pagan God Hades. Christ is pictured in a white robe and in a very lively manner here. The door-keeper of Hades is pictured as a black figure under his feet. Christ is shown resurrected and as the savior of people who believe in afterlife. He is pictured in a gold halo upon a blue background, and he pulls Adam and Eve into the sarcophagus.

Naos; the Koimesis mosaic; Mary's death.

The bearded figure at the left is John the Baptist who has informed them about the arrival of Christ; David and Solomon and a third , vague figure in an emperor's robe are in front of him. A crowd is seen behind them. At the left, the first figure in shepherd's clothes in his mother's sarcophagus is Abel. There is a parallel between him and Christ, both being

taken from Matthew 24, 25, from Mark 13, and from the Revelation.

Christ and Judgement Day

Christ is pictured on a throne and within a blue halo, and he is the center of the whole judgement scene. He has turned to the right slightly and he holds out his wounded hand as

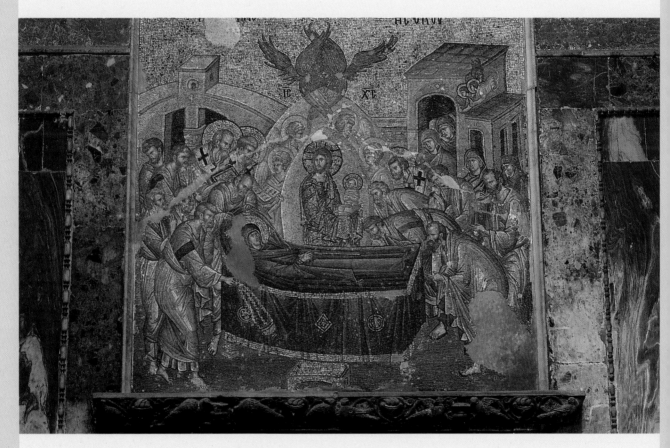

The Koimesis mosaic; Mary's death.

shepherds. The group of people in the background is lined up with the appropriate perspective, so that the mosaic gains depth.

The Last Judgement

This section of the church is a mausoleum chapel, and therefore, Doomsday and the Last Judgement are pictured in detail on the arch vault and at its bottom line. These scenes are

if he accepts or refuses the sanctification. Mary and John the Baptist beside him ask for benediction in the name of humanity. This scene is called the "deisis" in Byzantine art but it is a lot more crowded with the apostles and a group of people here.

Etimisia

This scene can be described as the preparation of the holy throne and is right

The Naos; mosaic of Jesus Christ.　　　　　*The Naos; mosaic of Virgin Mary.*

below the judgement scene cited above. The throne, on which Christ is to sit after resurrection, is covered with a dark cloth. Two cherubs guard it and are pictured right behind the throne. Adam and Eve have bent down to worship, and in the background we see a cross, a barbed crown, a lance and a sponge, the symbols of Christ's suffering. The source of this scene are the explanations in Hymns 88-85 and 15.

The weighing of the Souls

This scene is under the Etimisia and its key figure, the balance, is hung under the throne. Two angels at the left weigh the souls on that balance, and a naked figure in front of them waits for his turn. A crowded group waiting is at the right. The ones at the front have been found guilty and they proceed to the red fire lake at the side.

The Fire River and the Fire Lake

The fire river, which is born under Christ's feet, enlarges toward the pendant and becomes a fire lake. Faint figures are seen burning in the lake. The little black figure, which represents Satan, directs the guilty souls to the lake and pushes them in. We do not know the identity of the people who have dived halfway into the fire lake right above.

The Snail of Heaven

In the scene right at the center of the vault, we observe a winged angel with flying skirts who carries a spiral form which looks like a snail. This figure represents the rolled up world which gets ready for the judgement day. The sun, the moon and the stars send out beams of light.

The Choir of Selected People

Four groups of people are seen at the lower end of the vault. The identities of these people, who are across Christ in heaven, are written on their clothes or at the sides. Information about the figures who are on the clouds are also given either on their clothes or on the inscriptions above them.

The Choir of the Priests

This choir is composed of twenty-four persons with red or black crosses on their clothes.

The Choir of Holy Men

The figures on the long cloud at the west of the vault are dressed as monks. The apostles wear monks' dresses here with three of them at the front and the rest at the back.

The Choir of Prophets

They have knelt down with opened up hands, and they are dressed in the traditional "kimatson". We observe King Solomon and David with their crowns on their heads.

The Land and the Seas Deliver the Dead

The scene at the south-west of the vault is taken from Revelation 20:13 where the following is written: And the sea gave her dead; and death and the world of the dead revealed their dead too.

The dead who hear the angels' bugles enliven and rise from land and sea. The bugle of the angel at the left dives into the sea where it is heard by the dead underneath. We observe human pieces coming out of the fish mouths. The other angel awakens the dead on land.

The Rich Man is in Hell and the Beggar Lazarus is on Abraham's Lap

These two relevant themes taken from Luke 16 are painted on pendants facing each other. The rich man used to feed himself everyday and live in all richness. And he refused to help Lazarus who had come to his house. The naked picture in this mosaic burns in the fire; his face is tilted towards the left and he talks to Abraham (Luke 16:24). Money which has spilled out of the pouch is seen at the rich man's feet.

Lazarus the Beggar on Abraham's Lap

The good soul is in heaven, and is protected by Abraham. They are pictured on a white background and among flowers in

General view of the Paraklession.

Virgin Mary with angels at the dome of the Parreklesion.

heaven. Abraham sits on a throne and hugs Lazarus with his right arm. Lazarus is shown as a young child. There is a group of souls behind the throne, and they face each other.

The Angel and A Soul

This scene at the north-west of the dome vault is disputable. The angel has turned towards Christ in the judgement day and put his right hand on the naked figure's head who begs for mercy with opened up hands. This theme is unusual for Byzantine iconography. Some art historians think, that the scene has been added by the artist, and that the naked figure symbolizes Metokides. The angel, then, is put there to show, that Metokides is to be protected by the angel at the judgement day. Still some other art historians argue, that this scene is closely related to the other two scenes, and that it tells of the angel carrying Lazarus' soul to Abraham's lap.

Punishment of the Damned

The mosaics, which display the damned souls suffering in hell, have been separated from each other by the use of contrasting background colors. The contours of the figures painted on dark backgrounds which look like a chess board have been emphasized with black lines.

Receiving Those Who Go To Heaven

The scene which decorates the "tympanon" wall is made up of two parts. We see the processional of priests, martyrs and church fathers headed by St. Peter at the left. St. Peter holds the key of the heaven's door. At the other side, we observe a man holding a cross and ushering the new-comers in. Mary sits on a throne at the side and is surrounded by angels. There is a yellow stone which symbolizes the door of heaven in between, and the door is guarded by a cherub.

The dome of the Paraklesion

Maria Theodokos is pictured with the Child on her lap at the center of the dome. Twelve angels are placed between the dome strips and four of them hold spheres which symbolize the world. These are the archangels Michael, Gabriel, Uriel and Raphael. The rest of the angels have bibles in their hands. All the figures are successfully drawn. The bands which separate the figures from one another are richly decorated. In Byzantine art, inner decorations are made according to certain rules dictated by the art of painting: The pendants are usually filled with angels who bring the messages of God to mankind, and the cupolas symbolize the heavens. But in the Chora, authors and poets, who have written about Virgin Mary, are seen in the pendants.

The authors and poets are pictured at their writing desks, each one occupying a separate pendant. We observe St. Cosmos, St. Damascene, St. Joseph, St. Theophanes and Melchizedek, the king of Salem, among the authors in the pendants.

Mary Eleusia

This is another type of Virgin Mary portrait. She hugs the Child lovingly with her cheek upon his but she does not look at Christ. She looks absently in the distance as if she knows what will befall him and she has a sad expression.

The Church Fathers
The Tombs
The Resurrection of Jairus' Daughter

This scene, which is on the Bera vault, is decribed in the gospels of Mark, Luke and Matthew in detail. Jesus holds the dead girl by the hand and raises her softly. The bewilderment of her parents and the servants around the bed is seen clearly.

Jacob's Ladder

Two scenes concerning Jacob are seen at the lower end of the northern pendant. The first one is told in Genesis 28:12 of the Bible as such: And he dreamt and there was a ladder on the earth and his head reached the skies and God's angels went up and down the ladder. And God stopped on him and spoke:

Fresco of the Last Judgement.

Jacob dreamt of a ladder where there were angels and Mary holding the Child.

Jacob is the beardless young man at the bottom left. He leans on the rocks and sleeps, holding his head with one hand and his coat with the other. His cane is in front of him. Two of the four angels on the ladder behind him are looking back, and the other two extend their arms toward Mary who stands on top of the ladder. Jacob talking to the angels is told in Genesis 32:21: And Jacob was left alone and a man wrestled with him till daybreak. This scene is interpreted as such: Jacob has wrestled with God's angel, that is, he has come face to face with God. A young and beardless Jacob and the angel are pictured wrestling.

Carrying the Chest With the Imperial Decree

This scene is told in Kings 8:1-6: Then, Solomon gathered all the old men of Israel and the leaders of the Serbs.

He gathered them near King Solomon in Jerusalem in order to bring the chest from David's city of Sion. The figures who carry the chest wrapped up in a violet cloth are shown walking to the right. The buildings, which can be observed among the rocks in the background, represent Sion.

General view of the Parreklesion.

Christ brings Adam and Eve out of Hell.

John the Baptist, David and Solomon.

Detail from the fresco on Anastasis.

Carrying the Holy Candlestick

Exit 16:33 and Exit 25:31: And Moses spoke to Aaron and said: Take a pitcher and put "man" in it and place it at the priest's disposal, so that it can be kept for the generations to come. There are two figures in the scene which we see on the vault. The one at the left carries a seven-armed candlestick, and the other one carries the pitcher at the end of a rod.

Solomon and the People of Israel

King Solomon at the right is shown in the Byzantine imperial robe of purple and with a crown. He is in a walking position but his head is turned backwards facing the people of Israel. He has a Bible and a cane. The rocks and the trees in the background are put there to give the picture a perspective.

Placing the Holy chest in its Place

Two priests at the front are placing the chest on a throne which is decorated with pieces of cloth and medals. We see the temple door at the left and the people of Israel are waiting before it. The arch at the back gives depth to the composition. God's light which comes from the right illuminates the scene and cherubs at the back of the throne guard it.

The Oracle of Ishiah

Ishiah 37: 36: And God's angel appeared and hit hundred eighty five people at the Assyrian encampment and when men rose early in the morning, they were all dead.

The events during the siege of Jerusalem by the Assyrian king Sanherib are told here. The angel with a sword in his hand is the key figure of the picture. His sharp movement swings his cape. The Assyrian soldiers under his feet are smaller in size than the key figures. The door to Jerusalem can be observed in the background and the figure at the left is Ishiah. "The angel of God has come

Detail from the dome of the Parreklesion.　　　　*Fresco of Virgin Mary in the Parreklesion.*

and hit the Assyrians" can be read on the paper he holds.

Aaron and His Sons

Although its full explanation is not known, this picture is accepted to show Aaron and his sons, who were sanctified priests, make votive offerings at the altar which bore the holy chest.

Moses and the Burning Bush

This is one of the two pictures in the paraklesion which are on Moses.

Exit 3:2: And the angel of God appeared to him in the fire at the center of a bush and the bush was burning in the fire but it did not disappear. The picture is ruined and therefore, the flying angel amid the flames and the fire between him and Moses are hardly distinguished. Moses extends his left hand to the angel. Virgin Mary and Child are seen in

another bush at the other corner. This picture has two phases; Moses, who wears a red dress at the bottom, is taking out his shoe. His shoe is already out. Although the picture is in a bad condition, his hands unlacing the othre shoe can be observed. A group of animals can be seen in the front and the scene's description in the Bible is given in the background.

Exit 3:5: And he said: Do not come near, take off your shoes because the earth on which you stand is holy soil.

Moses Cannot Look at God in the Face

This picture is the continuation of the previous one. It is made in a narrow place at the foot of the vault. Moses has turned to the right, holds his cane in his hand, lifts up his right hand as if he wants to hide his face, and cannot look at Mary and Christ who are in the burning bush at the right.

The Fethiye Mosque

The building, which is called the Fethiye Mosque today, used to be one of the most prominent Byzantine churches in İstanbul. It is a complex which was erected on the fifth hill of the city overlooking the shores of the Golden Horn and the Asian side.

This building was a monastery church called Pammakaristos ("very very happy") after an attribute of Virgin Mary.

Although the central building was built in the mid-Byzantine age, the present church was erected by the nephew of Emperor Michael VIII Paleologus (1261-1282), Prostratos Michael Glabas Tarkhaniotes in 1292-94 after the Latin Invasion (The Dynastry of the Lascarids 1204-1261). The identity of its founder is given in an epigram by Manuel Philes. After Michael Glabas' death, his widow, Maria, had a Parreklesion (church chapel) built in the south of the church in 1315 which was dedicated to Jesus Christ. The tombs of Michael and Maria used to be in the Parreklesion. The outer

The Mosque of Fethiye; inner view.

corridors which enfold the building like a horse hoof must have been built after 1350.

This building was a Ladies' Monastery until 1455. The Patriarch turned this building into a Patriarchate in 1455 after he movel the establishment from the Apostles' Church. It remained so until 1586 when Sultan Murad III took it from the Christins and turned it into a mosque with the name, Fethiye Mosque.

The mosque was restored in 1846 under Sultan Abdülmecid. It was restored again in 1938-40 whereby its front was cleared of the plaster.

Although the central building was erected in 1292-94, and the cemetery chapel in the south and the galleries were built later on, the church looks like a unified building.

The mosque of Fethiye; mosaic of Jesus Christ.

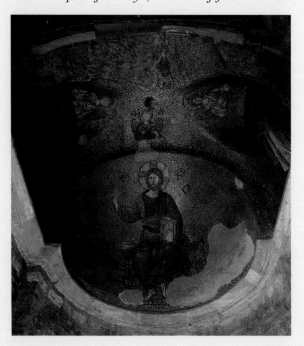

The Mosque of Fethiye; general outer view.

The Mosque of Fethiye inner view.

İmrahor İlyas Bey Mosque

Built in 454-463, this church is the oldest Byzantine monument which has reached our day. It is the church of a monastery built by Patriarch Studios and dedicated to John the Baptist.

It was converted to a mosque in the Turkish age and called the İmrahor İlyas Bey Mosque.

It is in Yedikule and is in a pretty bad state. It has a protruding absis, three nave, galleries and narthexes.

It has been ruined and restored many times during its history. The dome of the basilica has fallen down but the green marble columns inside, its floor mosaics of the XIII. century, and its composite capitals have reached our day.

The Small St. Sophia Mosque.

The Church of Sergios and Bacchus

This church which is situated at the seaside in the district of Sultanahmet was transformed into a mosque, called Küçük Ayasofya Small St. Sophia, in the Turkish age. Emperor Justinian had it built adjacent to the palace in 527-536. The emperor was believed to have dreamt of St. Sergios and then dedicated the church to him. The two-floored building has a central plan like that of San Vitale in Ravenna. The names of the emperor and his "very pious" wife Theodora can be read on the strip which is between the floors, and which enfolds the whole building's interior.

This church building is a square on the outside and an octagon in the inside. It is in a pretty well shape today, and its only supplement is the last congregation place.

The İmrahor İlyas Bey Mosque.

The St. Irene Church; an outside view.

St. Irene Church

This building, which is in the courtyard of the Topkapı Palace, was once the first Turkish museum. It is a concert hall today. The church was build on the ruins of an old temple of Aphrodite to celebrate "Holy Peace" during the reign of Constantine I.

It was the most prominent church until the construction of St. Sophia, and came to be called "Megala ecclessia" together with it later on. The second religious council met here in 381 and it was ruined like St. Sophia during the "Nika Revold" in 532.

It was restored by emperor Justinian and kept on being the second most important church throughout history.

It was restored again by Leo VIII. after it was demolished by an earthquake.

St. Irene was used as a military depot in the Turkish age because it was right next to the Topkapı Palace.

There is a huge mosaic cross in the semi-dome of the absistand a mosaic inscription from the Bible in the arch-vault.

Since only crosses were allowed in the churches during the Iconoclastic Period, it may well be, that the crosses were made then.

Concert at the St. Irene Church.

The Atik Mustafa Pasha Mosque (St. Thekla).

The Church of the Acatalepthos Monastery

This church is in the district of Süleymaniye in İstanbul, and was turned into a mosque with the name of Kalenderhane Mosque in the Turkish age. It is generally accepted to be the former Acatalepthos Church although its precise history is not known and is dated back to 1086. It was restored by a Turkish-American team in recent years.

The restorations made in the Ottoman period have changed the shape of the absis and the dome but the building still reflects its unique architecture.

The Kalenderhane Mosque.

The Fenari İsa Mosque.

The Lips Monastery

The Turkish name of the building on the Vatan Avenue is Fenari İsa Mosque. This edifice, which is composed of two adjacent naves and an L-shaped corridor, is still a mosque today.

The first building in the north was erected by a Byzantine nobleman called Constantine Lips in 908 and was dedicated to Virgin Mary. This complex was restored after the Latin conquest was overthrown and a southern church was added to the complex which was then dedicated to John the Baptist.

The inner hallways were built during the XIV. century.

The Lips Monastery lived through a number of fires and the last restoration took place in 1907. It was studied and restored quite often compared to the other Byzantine monuments.

The Rose Mosque (St. Theodosia).

The Mosque of Bodrum.

St. Theodosia

It is in Cibali at the shores of the Golden Horn, and its original name and history are not known. Still, the church was called St. Theodosia since the XIV. century.

Theodosia died during an upheaval in the Iconoclastic Period hereby a Jesus icon was demolished and was canonized.

After the Turkish conquest, it was turned into a mosque, restored and named Gül (Rose) Mosque. This building has a totally different dome structure compared to the classical Byzantine style.

Myrailaton

This building dates back to the mid-Byzantine era and is ruined today. It is in a street parallel to the Koska Avenue in Laleli and has served as a mosque in the Turkish age, called the Bodrum Mosque. It was builty by Romanus I Lecapenus in the first half of the X. century. Romanus Lecapenus was not an emperor but claimed coregency. The emperor of the age was Contastine VII Porphyrogenitus (913-959) who indulged in scientific work and left the affairs of state to Lecapenus. This building was burned in 1911 and got restored in recent years.

The Church Mosque of Zeyrek.

Pantocrator Monastery Church

This church is a part of a large religious complex built by John II Comnenus and his spouse Irene, whose portraits can be seen in St. Sophia. The church was composed of three buildings.

The cemetery chapel built for the emperor's family was between the northern and southern buildings. Rich floor mosaics and window panes have been found in the southern church.

Only the cisterns of the church exist today but we know, that it also had a library and a hospital once. This building is on the Atatürk Boulevard and was given the name Zeyrek Kilise Mosque in the Turkish.

The Church Mosque of Zeyrek; an inner view.

St. Theodore

This church is called Vefa Kilise Mosque and we do not have clear evidence on its Byzantine past.

The central part of the buildings is accepted to have been built during the mid-Byzantine age, and the outer narthex is thought to have been added during the last phase of the empire. The name, St. Theodore, was presimably found appropriate for the church.

The St. Adreas Church

This church bears the name Koca Mustafa Pasha Mosque. It is an outstanding example of the churches with corridors but its walls were covered in the Turkish age, therefore, its plan is barely visible. This building dates back to the XII. or XIII. century and was built by a lady called Theodorra Raouleina.

The City-Walls of Istanbul

İstanbul has been surrounded by city-walls four times since its foundation. The Megarans were the first to build the initial city-walls in the seventh century B.C. Septimus Severus (193-211) had the first city-walls destroyed after he conquered the city in 196 B.C, and had a second row of city-walls built which was named after him. Both of these city-walls used to encircle the first city settlement around Sarayburnu (the Seraglio Point). The third belt of city-walls was erected by Constantine I who made İstanbul the second capital of the Roman Empire. The third row was between Cerrahpaşa running to the Sea of Marmara and Fener running to the Golden Horn. The last belt of city-walls was begun in the era of Theodosius II (412-413) and was almost complete in 422 B.C. They enlarged the city as far as Yedikule towards the Sea of Marmara and as far as Ayvansaray towards the Golden Horn. The previous city-walls cited above had crumbled away as early as Byzantine rule.

İstanbul's city-walls are one of the longest defence establishments of Europe with their total length of 21 kilometers. They have more than fifty portals and over three hundred bastions. The city-walls of İstanbul are usually divided into three sections, the first one being the land walls of 7 kilometers between the Sea of Marmara and the Golden Horn, the second one being the city-walls of the Golden Horn which are 5 kilometers long, and the third one called the sea walls as long as 8 kilometers

The land walls of İstanbul in the Byzantine Age.

The land walls of İstanbul.

along the coast of the Sea of Marmara. The land walls are arranged according to a three-lined plan. The ditches come first at the outer face followed by the line of frontal walls and finally, the last and inner walls are placed behind the frontal row. The inner walls are 3-8 meters wide and 11-13 meters high. The bastions are attached to the walls with a distance of 50-75 meters in between them. There are 96 towers on the land walls. The average altitude of the towers, which stick out 10-11 meters from the wall, is 24 meters. The towers usually have two or three floors, and are roofed with either a dome or an arch-vault. Some of the towers of the city-walls are especially renowned. One of these is the inner castle called Yedikule, and the other one is the marble tower at the side of the Sea of Marmara, which has served as a prison for a long time. The portals of the city-walls are just as important. They are classified in two groups which are called the main and the secondary portals. The secondary or side portals were used for military purposes. Their inner sides were covered with marble layers, and some of them had wooden wings coated with bronze. The most famous portals of the land walls bear the following names: Belgrad Kapısı (Belgrade Portal), Silivri Kapı, Topkapı (Cannon Portal), Sulukule Kapısı and Edirnekapı. The ones on the walls of the Golden Horn are: Balat Kapısı, Fener Kapısı and Zindankapı. And the most famous ones on the walls of Marmara are: Çatladıkapı, Kumkapı (Sand Portal) and Yenikapı (New Portal). Although the city-walls of İstanbul have been built by Byzantine emperors, the following Ottoman rule has preserved and restored them. The Ottomans have also opened up new portals and added buildings like mosques and mausoleums in their close vicinity. Some parts of the city-walls have become extinct in the last phases of the Ottoman Empire because of a lack of interest in them. The city-walls of İstanbul were put under monument protection after the foundation of the Republic. Numerous research and repair work has been done, the last one of which is going on steadily since 1986.